SANTA ANA PUBLIC LIBRARY

AR PTS: 0.5

YOKUTS

Big Buddy Books
An Imprint of Abdo Publishing
abdopublishing.com

Katie Lajiness

abdopublishing.com

Published by Abdo Publishing, a division of ABDO, PO Box 398166, Minneapolis, Minnesota 55439.
Copyright © 2017 by Abdo Consulting Group, Inc. International copyrights reserved in all countries. No part
of this book may be reproduced in any form without written permission from the publisher. Big Buddy Books™
is a trademark and logo of Abdo Publishing.

Printed in the United States of America, North Mankato, Minnesota.
062016
092016

**THIS BOOK CONTAINS
RECYCLED MATERIALS**

Cover Photo: Reprinted with the permission of the *Hanford Sentinel*, © 2014; Shutterstock.com.
Interior Photos: © Blue Lantern Studio/Corbis (p. 23); © CH Collection/Alamy (p. 26); © Christie's Images/Corbis
    (p. 16); Lee Foster/Alamy (p. 5); *Getty Images*: Rich Reid (p. 21); Reprinted with the permission of the *Hanford
    Sentinel*, © 2014 (p. 29); © iStockphoto.com (pp. 17, 27, 30); © NativeStock.com/AngelWynn (pp. 9, 13, 15, 17);
    Shutterstock.com (pp. 11, 19, 25).

Quote on page 30 from the *Hanford Sentinel*.

Coordinating Series Editor: Tamara L. Britton
Graphic Design: Adam Craven

Library of Congress Cataloging-in-Publication Data

Lajiness, Katie, author.
   Yokuts / Katie Lajiness.
Minneapolis, MN : ABDO Publishing Company, 2017. | Series:
   Native Americans
LCCN 2015050499 (print) | LCCN 2015051360 (ebook) | ISBN
   9781680782042 (print) | ISBN 9781680774993 (ebook)
Yokuts Indians--History--Juvenile literature. | Yokuts
   Indians--Social life and customs--Juvenile literature.
LCC E99.Y75 L28 2017 (print) | LCC E99.Y75 (ebook) | DDC
   970.004/974133--dc23
LC record available at http://lccn.loc.gov/2015050499

CONTENTS

AMAZING PEOPLE

Hundreds of years ago, North America was mostly wild, open land. Native American tribes lived on the land. They had their own languages and **customs**.

The Yokuts (YOH-kuhts) are one Native American tribe. They are known for their **ceremonies** and handmade crafts. Let's learn more about these Native Americans.

Did You Know?

The name *Yokuts* means "people."

The Yokuts continue to pass along their native customs. Women still weave their traditional baskets.

YOKUTS TERRITORY

Yokuts homelands were in what is now California. Some lived in the San Joaquin Valley. Other tribes lived at the base of the Sierra Nevada. The Yokuts had about 40 groups, all speaking the same language. Each had about 350 people, its own name, and territory. Yokuts tribes were separated into clans.

CANADA

UNITED STATES

YOKUTS HOMELANDS

CALIFORNIA

NEVADA

MEXICO

HOME LIFE

Yokuts people lived in houses shaped like ovals or cones. The frame was made of poles fashioned from young trees. Many were covered with tule, pine needles, or tarweed. Several homes were so large, up to ten families lived inside!

The frame's poles were tied together at the top to give the house its shape.

What They Ate

The Yokuts ate a wide range of foods. Men fished for salmon. They hunted deer, elk, and antelope. And, they caught birds such as geese, ducks, and quail.

Women collected berries, roots, and seeds, such as pine nuts and wild oats. They also gathered mussels and other shellfish.

Acorns were a common food. Women smashed acorns to make flour for baking bread.

DAILY LIFE

The Yokuts lived in villages. Each tribe had a chief. Many families lived in the same home.

They wore few clothes. Many people had **tattooed** faces and bodies. Men wore **loincloths**. Women wore aprons made from bark. Most young children did not wear clothes.

Each village had a sweathouse. Men gathered inside the hot building to sweat. Then they ran into a nearby stream to cool down.

13

In a Yokuts village, they traded goods with neighboring tribes. Fish, salt, seeds, and animal skins were popular goods to trade. In return, they received acorns, rabbit-skin blankets, shells, and beads.

Yokuts men and women had different jobs. The men made tools. They also hunted and fished. Women made pottery and baskets. Cooking and caring for the children were women's jobs. Parents taught their children these life skills.

Yokuts women carried their children in cradleboards while they did daily tasks.

MADE BY HAND

The Yokuts made many objects by hand. They often used natural materials. These arts and crafts added beauty to everyday life.

Baskets
Yokuts women made baskets with geometric patterns. These baskets held food and water, among other uses.

Boats

Yokuts men made boats out of tule. This type of boat is known as a balsa.

Clothes

Women wove plants such as nettle (*left*) and hemp into skirts. They also decorated headbands with seeds and feathers.

Spirit Life

Shamans were important to the Yokuts religion. They led ceremonies and rituals.

The rattlesnake ceremony took place every spring. Women wove baskets to fill with rattlesnakes. The shamans danced around the baskets. They believed this would protect them from snakebites.

In the 1870s, many Yokuts began to attend Ghost Dances. They believed these ceremonies would bring their dead family members back to life.

The Yokuts believed rattlesnakes were the helpers of the spirit world. These snakes were said to watch the tribes and report back to the gods.

STORYTELLERS

Stories are important to the Yokuts. They were told for fun and to teach lessons. In the Yokuts's creation story, the world was once covered with water. A large eagle mixed mud with seeds to form the earth.

Thousands of years ago, the Yokuts told stories using cave drawings. They made the drawings with dirt, charcoal, and animal fat. Many of these drawings can still be seen today.

Fighting for Land

Throughout history, the Yokuts were generally a peaceful people. In 1772, the Spanish first met the Yokuts. They tried to make the Yokuts live like Europeans.

During the 1820s, Mexican settlers moved into the area. Again, the Yokuts fought for their freedom and land.

Spanish explorers arrived in California and forced Native Americans to adopt European ways of life. Over time, Yokuts learned to speak Spanish.

23

In 1848, the US government added California to the union. White settlers came and stole land from the Yokuts. As more people arrived, their tribal land gradually became smaller.

The next year, more settlers came to California. They were looking for gold. They believed gold would make them wealthy. Settlers killed many Yokuts and took more land.

More than 300,000 settlers came to California in search of gold. The Yokuts did not have enough power to protect their lands from the settlers.

BACK IN TIME

1833

Many Yokuts died from new sicknesses brought over by Europeans.

Early 1800s

Missionaries began to convert the Yokuts to Christianity.

1851

All of the Yokuts tribes were moved to reservations.

1873

The Tule River **Reservation** was established for the Yokuts. It covers nearly 85 square miles (220 sq km) in the Sierra Nevada.

1950s

Most Yokuts children were sent to public schools for Native Americans. They were told not to practice their **traditions**.

Late 1970s

About 325 Yokuts lived on the Tule River Reservation. And, about 100 lived on the Santa Rosa Rancheria.

THE YOKUTS TODAY

The Yokuts have a long, rich history. They are remembered for their woven baskets and stories.

Yokuts roots run deep. Today, the people have kept alive those special things that make them Yokuts. Even though times have changed, many people carry the **traditions**, stories, and memories of the past into the present.

Did You Know?

Today, about 4,000 Yokuts live in the United States.

Young Yokuts still gather at festivals to dance and practice their customs.

"We believe in living in rhythm and perfect harmony with the land.… We want to make sure our **culture** is passed on to future **generations**."

– Hector "Lalo" Franco, Director, Santa Rosa Rancheria Cultural and Historical Preservation Department

GLOSSARY

ceremony a formal event on a special occasion.

Christianity (krihs-chee-A-nuh-tee) a religion that follows the teachings of Jesus Christ.

culture (KUHL-chuhr) the arts, beliefs, and ways of life of a group of people.

custom a practice that has been around a long time and is common to a group or a place.

generation (jeh-nuh-RAY-shuhn) a single step in the history of a family.

loincloth a simple cloth worn by a man to cover his lower body.

missionary a person who travels to share his or her religious beliefs with others.

reservation (reh-zuhr-VAY-shuhn) a piece of land set aside by the government for Native Americans to live on.

ritual (RIH-chuh-wuhl) a formal act or set of acts that is repeated.

shaman a person who is believed to be able to use magic to heal sickness or see the future.

tattoo to mark the body with a picture or pattern by using a needle to put color under the skin.

tradition (truh-DIH-shuhn) a belief, a custom, or a story handed down from older people to younger people.

WEBSITES

To learn more about Native Americans, visit **booklinks.abdopublishing.com**. These links are routinely monitored and updated to provide the most current information available.

31

INDEX